LEARNING ABOUT
God

Lois Rock

Illustrated by Maureen Galvani

WARNER Faith

A Division of AOL Time Warner Book Group

Text by Lois Rock
Text copyright © 2003 by Lion Publishing
Illustrations copyright © 2002 Maureen Galvani

First U.S. Edition
First published in Great Britain in 2002 by Lion Publishing

ISBN 0-316-76697-6

10 9 8 7 6 5 4 3 2 1

Printed in Singapore

The text was set in Apollo MT, and the display type is Elroy and Fineprint.

Introduction: Who is God?

"God" is the name we Christians use for the One we worship. Why do we believe in God? How do we know anything about God? Here is what we might answer:

"The book of our faith, the Bible, tells us about God. It is a book written hundreds of years ago. It tells us the stories of people who believed in God long ago. We can learn from them.

"We also believe that God is our friend today. We believe God is close to us and helps us."

This book asks some everyday questions about God you might want to ask and lets us Christians give our reply.

1. How old is God?

The Bible says that God existed before the beginning of the world, but God is neither young nor old. God is the One who simply is.

God gave the world its beginning. He made the world and everything in it.

God made the sun and the moon and the stars.

God made the land and the sea.

God made the hills and the valleys. God made the trees and the flowers, the birds and the animals, the fish and the insects.

God made people. God gave us our beginning.

 We believe that God is the One who is forever, the One who gave this world its beginning.

2. Does God like the world?

The Bible says that God made a world that was very, very good.

Today we see many good and lovely things in the world:

creatures with wide and wonderful eyes,

windswept seas and white-crested waves where dolphins dance and dive,

fragile flowers, towering trees,

and millions and millions of people,
who are all special in different ways.

The Bible says that God is love, and that God loves the world
even more than a parent loves a child.

**We believe that God loves the world and takes
care of it.**

3. Has God noticed the bad things in the world?

Next to the Bible stories about God making the world is another story—about the bad things in the world.

In the beginning, the first people lived as happily as children in a paradise garden.

God warned them not to try to find
out about bad things.

One day a cunning snake
came along. It told them not
to worry, but to do the very
thing that would make them
wise like God. So they
disobeyed God.

Then they noticed that
everything changed.

They were no longer close
friends with God. Their home
was no longer the paradise garden,
but an unkind world. There they were
going to have to work and work until the day
they died.

**We believe that God knows all about the bad
things in the world that make people sad.**

4. Can't God fix the world?

The Bible tells about some of the things God has done to fix the world.

In the Bible are laws that tell us the right way to live — laws about loving God and about loving one another.

In the Bible are stories that tell us how much God loves us and forgives us.

In the Bible are stories of Jesus. We believe that Jesus was God's Son who came to show us even more about how much God welcomes us as friends.

When we are friends with God, then everything is as right as it can be.

 We believe that God has done everything to make friends with us.

5. What does God look like?

No one knows what God looks like, but the Bible helps us know a bit about what He is like.

God is a loving caretaker — like a mother bird looking after her chicks.

God is strong—like a rock on which a person can be safe from danger.

God is a father in heaven.

God is love.

Do those words help build a picture of God?

In the Bible, we find words that help describe God.

6. Where does God live?

The Bible says that God lives in a place called heaven.

But if God is the One who simply is, then heaven is the place that simply is.

That means that heaven is bigger than the whole universe. No wonder people often look up toward the wide sky when they speak of heaven.

But even though heaven is bigger than we can imagine, God is closer to us than the air we breathe.

 We believe that God is everywhere and always with us.

7. What does God do?

The Bible says that God takes care of the world.

God is in charge of the sun, the wind and the rain, the seasons and the harvests.

God is in charge of everything. Even if bad things may seem to win for a while, God and His goodness are stronger in the end.

We who love God see all things working together for the good.

We believe that God takes care of everything.

8. Does God watch everything people do?

We believe that God is the One who simply is, and that God is invisibly everywhere and knows everything that happens.

So we believe that we are always close to God, who is good...

and loving...

and forgiving.

 We believe that God watches over us with love.

9. Does God take sides?

The Bible says that God is on the side of what is good and right.

God is on the side of people who are poor and unhappy.

God is on the side of people who get treated unfairly. God is on the side of people who sometimes feel that nobody wants to be friends with them.

The Bible says that God cares even for the littlest sparrow. God cares for us even more.

 We believe that God cares for everyone, especially those with no one else to help them.

10. Can people talk to God?

The Bible tells of people long ago who talked to God by praying. We who believe in God today also talk to God by praying.

Sometimes we say prayers aloud.

Sometimes we think them quietly.

Sometimes we write
them down.

Sometimes we simply sigh
because we cannot think of the
right words.

God knows what every prayer
means. God listens to them all.

 **We believe that God listens to our prayers.**

11. Does God speak to people?

We who believe in God listen carefully to what is in the Bible.

We believe it tells us about things God has said and things God has done.

We also pray to God and believe that God answers our prayers.

Sometimes the answer is in the things that happen after we pray.

Sometimes the answer is like a loud thought that stays with us.

Sometimes the answer is something said by another person.

We believe that God speaks to us in many different ways.

12. What will happen to God in the end?

The Bible says that God is the One who simply is—

the One who was before the beginning
of the world,

the One who will be after the end
of the world.

And when we die and leave this world, we will be safe in the love of the One who simply is.

Forever.

We believe that God is for always.

Who is God?

1. We believe that God is the One who is forever, the One who gave this world its beginning.

2. We believe that God loves the world and takes care of it.

3. We believe that God knows all about the bad things in the world that make people sad.

4. We believe that God has done everything to make friends with us.

5. In the Bible, we find words that help describe God.

6. We believe that God is everywhere and always with us.

7. We believe that God takes care of everything.

8. We believe that God watches over us with love.

9. We believe that God cares for everyone, especially those with no one else to help them.

10. We believe that God listens to our prayers.

11. We believe that God speaks to us in many different ways.

12. We believe that God is for always.